SCIENCE
IS EVERYWHERE

OUT OF THIS WORLD

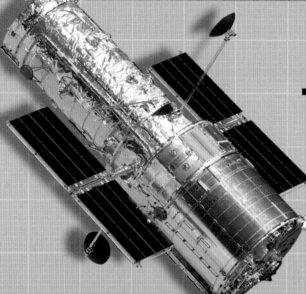

The planets and the Universe

Rob Colson

WAYLAND

Published in paperback in Great
Britain in 2019 by Wayland
Copyright © Hodder and Stoughton, 2017

Wayland
An imprint of Hachette
Children's Group
Part of Hodder and Stoughton
Carmelite House
50 Victoria Embankment
London EC4Y 0DZ

Executive editor: Adrian Cole
Produced by Tall Tree Ltd
Written by: Rob Colson
Designer: Ben Ruocco

ISBN: 978 1 5263 0460 5
10 9 8 7 6 5 4 3 2 1

An Hachette UK Company
www.hachette.co.uk
www.hachettechildrens.co.uk

Printed and bound in China

The website addresses (URLs) included
in this book were valid at the time of
going to press. However, it is possible
that contents or addresses may have
changed since the publication of this book.
No responsibility for any such changes
can be accepted by either the author or
the Publisher.

t-top, b-bottom, l-left, r-right, c-centre,
front cover-fc, back cover-bc
All images courtesy of Dreamstime.com,
unless indicated:
Inside front NASA, ESA, and P. Crowther;
fc, bc Pablo631; fctc Photohare; fctr Tomas
Griger; fccl NASA; fccr Maxcortesiphoto;
fcb Alexmit; bctl Juliengrondin; bctr,
11tr NASA; bccl, 25tl, 31tr JWST/NASA;
1cl, 24l NASA; 4, 10c, b, 28t Alhovik;
6tl, 15c, 28bl Johan63; 6b, 14c NASA;
7c Manaemedia; 7b Kritchanut; 8c Peter
Hermes Furian; 9tc, 14cl, 27t Mexrix;
9t Bodrumsurf; 9b Rudall30; 11cl NASA;
11b Mzwonko; 12b NASA; 13tc Mishkacz;
13cl NASA; 13b Amy Ford; 14bl NASA;
15 shutterstock/Dundanim; 16tr NASA;
16-17b 7activestudio; 18 NASA; 5tl, 18br,
21tr Vectorlibellule; 19t Andreadonetti;
20t Creativemarc; 20-21c, 30tr Dedmazay;
23t NASA; 24c NASA; 26b NASA; 27tr
NASA; 27cl A-papantoniou; 27b NRAO/
AUI/NSF; 29b Siimsepp; 30tl NASA; 30bc
NASA; 32t Stylephotographs

Contents

The Solar System

Planet Earth is part of a family of planets, moons, asteroids and comets that all orbit the Sun, known as the solar system.

Mercury

Earth

Venus

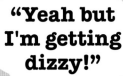
Mars

"Going around again?"

Saturn

"Yeah but I'm getting dizzy!"

Neptune

Jupiter

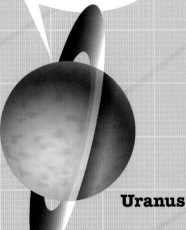
Uranus

The ecliptic
The eight planets are large, spherical bodies that follow regular orbits on a plane called the ecliptic.

Elliptical orbits

The planets do not orbit the Sun in circles, but in a regular oval shape called an **ellipse**.

Earth

a

b

Focus 1
(Sun)

a

b

Focus 2
(point in space)

At each point in a planet's orbit, the sum of the distances from each focus (**a + b**) is the same. One focus is the Sun, while the other is a point in empty space.

Our red neighbour

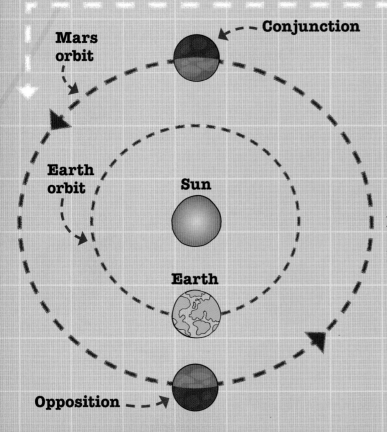

Conjunction

Mars orbit

Earth orbit

Sun

Earth

Opposition

The distance between the planets varies hugely depending on where they are in their orbits around the Sun. At its closest to Earth, Mars is **56 million kilometres** away, and appears to be very bright in the night sky. This is called **opposition** because Mars appears on the opposite side of Earth from the Sun. Earth and Mars are in opposition once every two years. Missions to Mars are launched at this time to minimise the length of the journey. At its farthest, Mars is up to **400 million kilometres** away, and is much less bright. This is called **conjunction** because Mars appears on the same side of Earth as the Sun.

Marking time

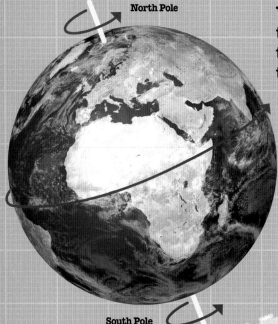

North Pole

South Pole

We measure the passing of time using units based on the movements of Earth, the Sun and the Moon.

One rotation, one orbit

Earth spins on an axis that goes through the poles. One full rotation of Earth relative to the Sun is equal to one day. A full orbit around the Sun is equal to one year.

The seasons

Earth's axis is tilted at an angle of 23 degrees. This means that the northern hemisphere is angled towards the Sun in June, giving the long, warm days of summer. In December, the northern hemisphere is angled away from the Sun, giving the short, cold days of winter. The reverse is true for the southern hemisphere.

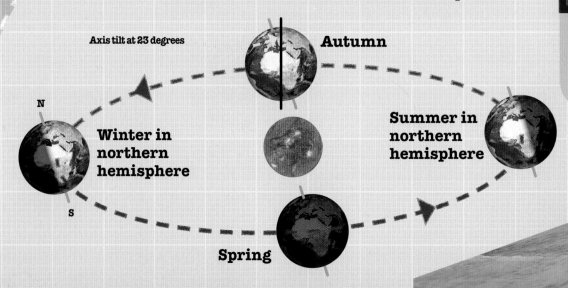

Axis tilt at 23 degrees

Autumn

N

Winter in northern hemisphere

S

Summer in northern hemisphere

Spring

LEAP YEARS

Most calendar years contain **365 days**, but a full orbit of Earth around the Sun is in fact equal to

365.2425 days.

To catch up, an extra day is added every

four years

to make a leap year. That makes an average of **365.25 days**, which is a little too long, so every **400 years, three leap years** are missed out.

29 FEBRUARY

Here is the formula for working out a leap year:

Is the year divisible by four?

YES Is the year divisible by 100?

NO not a leap year

YES Is the year divisible by 400?

NO is a leap year

YES is a leap year

NO is not a leap year

Can you work out when the next leap year is due?

Venus spins very slowly on its axis, meaning that it takes 243 Earth days to rotate once.

Venus orbits the Sun once every 225 Earth days, meaning that a Venusian day is longer than a Venusian year!

Shifting ground

The solid ground on which we walk is a hard, rocky crust about 40 km thick. The crust is made of pieces called tectonic plates, which float on hot liquid magma underneath.

Sliding plates

The **San Andreas Fault** lies at the **boundary** between the **Pacific plate** and the **North American plate**. The two plates regularly slide past each other, creating earthquakes.

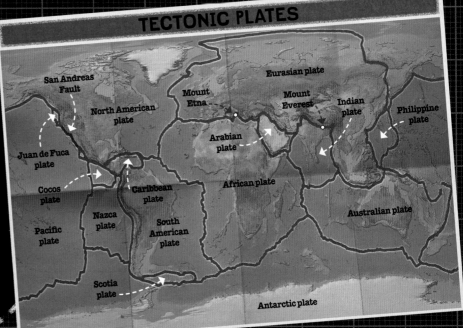

TECTONIC PLATES

San Andreas Fault

North American plate

Juan de Fuca plate

Cocos plate

Pacific plate

Nazca plate

Caribbean plate

South American plate

Scotia plate

Mount Etna

Arabian plate

African plate

Eurasian plate

Mount Everest

Indian plate

Philippine plate

Australian plate

Antarctic plate

Unpredictable quakes

In 1906, an earthquake struck **San Francisco**, which lies near the San Andreas Fault. It destroyed

80 per cent

of the city. Today, scientists monitor the fault and try to predict when and where the next 'big one' might occur.

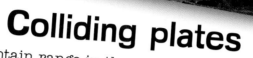

At the peak of Mount Everest in the Himalayas, the rock is made from marine limestone, which once lay at the bottom of the ocean.

Colliding plates

The highest mountain range in the world, **the Himalayas**, was formed by the collision of **two continental plates** about 50 million years ago. The Indian Plate collided with the Eurasian Plate, causing the rock to **fold upwards at the boundary.** The two plates are still pushing against one another, meaning that the mountains grow about **5 mm higher every year**.

Subducting plates

Where one plate is pushed underneath another, the plate being forced down is crushed and melted.

This is called a **subduction zone**, and often results in volcanoes, as molten magma pushes up to the surface. **Mount Etna** in Italy is an active volcano in a subduction zone, where the African plate is being pushed underneath the Eurasian plate.

"Quick, get the marshmallows."

Rocky dwarfs and gas giants

Mars

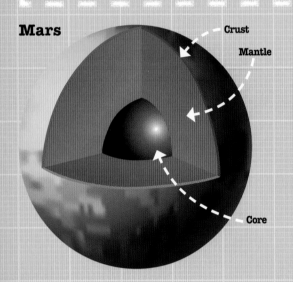

Crust

Mantle

Core

The rocky planets

The four planets closest to the Sun are small and rocky. They all have a **metallic core**, surrounded by a **liquid mantle**, with a **solid crust** on top.

Gas giants

Outside the rocky planets are the four gas giants. Under their gas surfaces are layers of **liquid** and a **rocky core**.

Jupiter

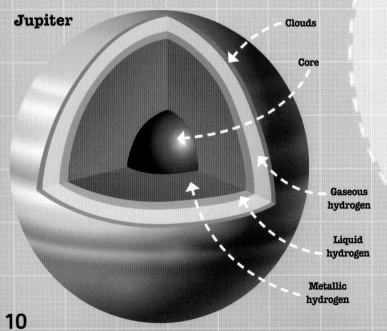

Clouds

Core

Gaseous hydrogen

Liquid hydrogen

Metallic hydrogen

Saturn's rings

From a distance, Saturn appears to be surrounded by a series of solid rings. The rings are made up of small pieces of **ice and rock,** up to the size of a large house, which are orbiting the planet at high speed. The rings are **thousands of kilometres wide**, but less than **100 metres thick**. Scientists are not sure how they formed, but they may be broken pieces of moons. Jupiter, Uranus and Neptune also have rings.

Neptune

Saturn

Uranus

Sun

Jupiter

Close-up of the
ring particles

Orbits of
planets

Gravitational pull

Finding Neptune

Each planet's orbit is affected by the gravitational pull of other planets. Uranus was discovered in 1781, and observations of its orbit suggested that another planet farther out was pulling on it. In 1846, French mathematician Urbain Le Verrier calculated where this planet should be, and Neptune was found almost exactly where he had predicted.

Stormy planet

Planets such as Earth that are surrounded by a gassy atmosphere all have weather systems, which sometimes develop into raging tropical storms.

Forming clouds

Weather systems are created because the Sun heats the surface unevenly. Where **the surface is warmer, the air expands** and rises, drawing cooler air in underneath. The air contains water in the form of the gas water vapour. **As it rises, the air cools** and some of this water vapour condenses into droplets of water to form clouds.

Tropical cyclones

Huge rotating storms called **tropical cyclones** form over warm oceans. Also called **hurricanes**, they cause torrential rain and high winds. Tropical cyclones always **rotate in the same direction**, depending on which hemisphere they form in. In the northern hemisphere, they rotate **anti-clockwise**, while in the southern hemisphere, they rotate **clockwise**. This is caused by the rotation of Earth.

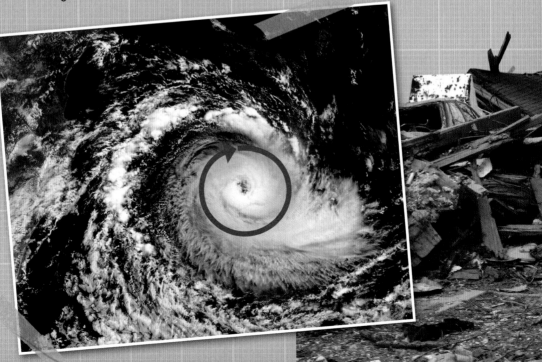

This tropical cyclone formed off the coast of Brazil in the southern hemisphere. It is rotating clockwise.

Condensation level

Air warms and expands, then rises and cools

Surface warms

TRY THIS

Earth is heated unevenly by the Sun because some surfaces reflect more heat than others. The snowy poles reflect more than half of the Sun's heat, while the oceans reflect less than 10 per cent. To see this difference, take two glasses and wrap one with white paper and the other with black paper. Fill the glasses with water and leave them in sunlight for a couple of hours. Using a thermometer, measure the temperature of the water in each glass.

The Great Red Spot could swallow Earth up whole.

Many huge storms form on the surface of Jupiter. The largest, called the **Great Red Spot**, has been raging for more than 300 years. Its winds reach more than

600 km/h.

Hurricane Katrina in 2005 caused massive devastation and destruction to residential homes along the Gulf coast in America.

The Moon

The Moon is Earth's only natural satellite. It orbits Earth once every 29.5 days, a period known as a lunar month.

Phases of the Moon

The Moon does not give off any light, so what we see from Earth is sunlight reflected off the Moon. Half of the Moon is always lit by the Sun. As the Moon orbits Earth, the portion of the lit side that we can see changes and the Moon appears to change shape. These are called the phases of the Moon.

New Moon

Violent birth

The chemical composition of rocks brought back from the Moon's surface matches that of rocks on Earth, and scientists think that the Moon may once have been part of Earth. It is thought that a Mars-sized planet, called **Theia**, collided with Earth **4.5 billion years ago**, sending out debris that formed the Moon.

"Whoa, did you not see me?"

Tidal force

Tides are the daily rise and fall of the oceans caused by the gravitational pull of the Moon and the Sun.

Spring tide

When the Moon and Sun are lined up, there is a large tide called a spring tide. This occurs near a full Moon and a New Moon.

When the Moon is at right angles to the Sun, there is a much smaller tide, called a neap tide. This occurs near the first and last quarter moons.

Neap tide

Last Quarter

Full Moon

First Quarter

TRY THIS

We always see the same side of the Moon from Earth, which means that the Moon rotates once every orbit. To see this, stick a toothpick into an orange. This is your 'Moon'. Ask a friend to stand still and be 'Earth', while you walk around them holding your 'Moon' with the toothpick always pointing towards 'Earth'. You will have to rotate your 'Moon' as you walk around 'Earth'.

The Sun's diameter is about

400 times greater

than that of the Moon, but the Sun is also about

400 times farther away.

This means that they appear roughly the same size from Earth. Occasionally, the Moon entirely blocks the Sun, an event called a solar eclipse.

Burning balls of gas

Stars, such as our Sun, are balls of hot gas that give off huge amounts of energy, produced by nuclear reactions deep below the surface.

The Hubble Space Telescope captured this image of a star-forming cloud of dust 7,000 light years away, which has been dubbed the **'Pillars of Creation'**.

Life cycle of the Sun

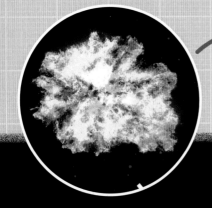

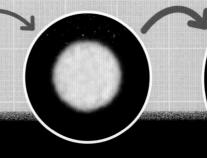

Our Sun was born about **4.6 billion years ago** from an immense cloud of dust called a **stellar nebula**. Gravity pulled the dust together into a hot, shining clump burning at more than **10 million degrees Celsius**.

Nuclear reactions inside the Sun fuse hydrogen atoms to make **helium atoms**, and this releases energy. Hydrogen is the **'fuel'** that keeps the Sun shining, and there is enough left to keep it shining for another **5 billion years**.

Near the end of its life, the Sun will swell up to become a **red giant**.

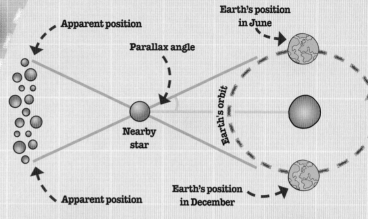

Stretch your arm out in front of you and hold your thumb upwards. Close your left eye, then your right, then your left again. **How much does your thumb's position appear to change against the background?**

Now do the same thing, but with your thumb close to your face. How much more does the thumb seem to shift when you switch eyes?

Measuring distances

Determining the **distance of stars** is one of the most difficult problems in astronomy. Astronomers can calculate the distance of nearby stars using a **method called parallax**. They measure the star's position once, then measure it again six months later, when Earth is on the **opposite side of its orbit** around the Sun. The change in the star's position against a background of more distant stars shows how far away it is.

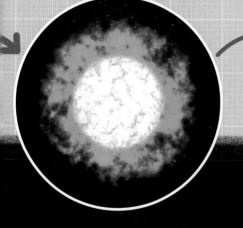

The Sun will end its life as a **planetary nebula**, throwing off its outer layers as its **fuel runs out**.

When the planetary nebula has dispersed, the hot core will be left behind. This core, called a **white dwarf**, will gradually cool over billions of years.

Occasional visitors

Comets are small objects that spend most of their time in the outer reaches of the solar system, far from our sight. Occasionally, a comet comes near to the Sun and we see it in the night sky, trailing its spectacular tail.

Rosetta

Dirty snowballs

In 2014, NASA's **Rosetta space craft** landed on Comet 67P/Churyumov–Gerasimenko, following an **eight-year journey** through space. It sent back photographs and information about the make-up of the comet. It was found to have a dry, rocky surface, but scientists believe that there is ice beneath the crust, and comets have been described as 'dirty snowballs'.

Philae lander

Comet

"Can I get a lift back?"

Forming a tail

As a comet approaches the Sun, its surface is heated and dust and gas melt or boil. This material surrounds the comet in a **fuzzy, glowing coma**. Some of the material is blown away from the comet to form a tail. While the solid nucleus of the comet may be only a few kilometres across, the coma can puff up to be as big as the Sun, while the tail can stretch for millions of kilometres.

A comet's tail always points away from the Sun. It is blown by the solar wind, a flow of energy given off by the Sun.

Coma

Dust tail

Gas tail

Comets follow huge elliptical orbits around the Sun and some of them return at regular intervals. Halley's comet passes Earth once every 76 years. Halley's comet appeared in the year 1066, just before the Battle of Hastings in England. Many people took its appearance to be a bad omen, and the comet appears on the Bayeux Tapestry, which was made after the battle, with people looking to the sky in horror.

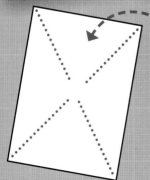

TRY THIS

What you need:
A piece of paper, two long strips of shiny tape, sticky tape, a straw, a blow dryer, scissors

1. Cut slits in the paper from each corner (see left).
2. Lay the strips over the slits to form an 'X' and tape them across the middle.
3. Crumple the paper into a ball, making sure that the strips are on the outside.
4. Poke a hole in the comet and insert the straw to hold it. Have a friend hold the dryer and switch it on. This will be your solar wind. Walk towards the wind holding your comet, and see how the tail moves.

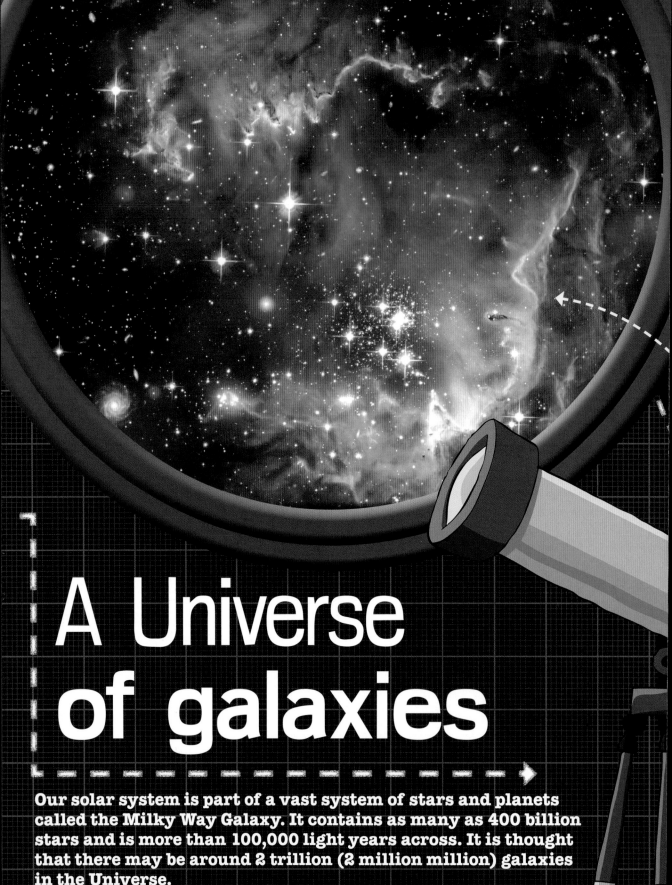

A Universe of galaxies

Our solar system is part of a vast system of stars and planets called the Milky Way Galaxy. It contains as many as 400 billion stars and is more than 100,000 light years across. It is thought that there may be around 2 trillion (2 million million) galaxies in the Universe.

Spiral galaxy

The Milky Way is in a spiral shape with huge curling arms. We are located in one of the spiral arms, and we see this arm as a milky strip of stars across the sky. The whole galaxy rotates once every 250 million years, a period called a cosmic year.

"I know it's big, but I didn't see it!"

Direction of rotation

Solar system

The **Large Magellanic Cloud** is a small galaxy 200,000 light years away that is visible to the naked eye from the Southern Hemisphere.

Black hole

Black hole

At the centre of every galaxy is a **huge black hole**. Black holes are regions in space that have such a **strong gravitational pull** that nothing can escape from them. We cannot see inside a black hole because even light cannot escape from its gravity. An astronaut falling feet-first towards a black hole would experience stronger and stronger gravity. Eventually, the gravity would **increase** so rapidly that the astronaut's feet would be pulled much more strongly than their head and their body would be stretched out like spaghetti. Astronomers call this

spaghettification.

An **expanding** Universe

Our Universe is expanding at an ever-increasing rate. The galaxies themselves stay the same size, held together by gravity, but the space in between the galaxies is getting bigger.

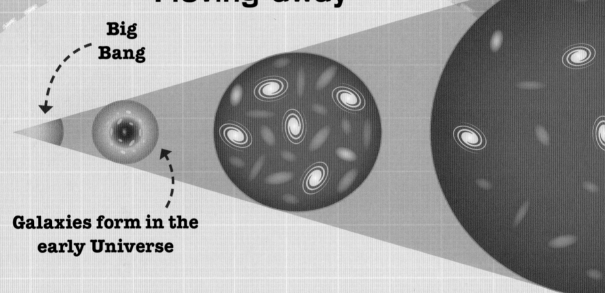

Moving away

Big Bang

Galaxies form in the early Universe

In the 1920s, American astronomers **Vesto Slipher** (1875–1969) and **Edwin Hubble** (1889–1953) discovered that all but the nearest galaxies were moving away from us. The **farther away** the galaxy was, the faster it was moving. Hubble realised that this means that the Universe is **expanding**.

Since the Universe is expanding, it must have been **smaller** in the past. Scientists have calculated that the Universe began from a single point about **13.7 billion years ago**, an event known as **the Big Bang**. In the late 1990s, scientists discovered that the Universe's expansion is speeding up. This accelerated expansion was a surprise, and is caused by an unknown source of energy. This mysterious energy has been dubbed **'dark energy'**, but currently nobody knows what it is.

Collision course

The nearest major galaxy to us, **Andromeda**, is actually on its way towards us, pulled by gravity. In about 3.75 billion years, the night sky above Earth will look like this, with Andromeda clearly visible as it collides with the Milky Way.

Galaxies are carried farther apart as the Universe expands

TRY THIS

In an expanding Universe, the farther away a galaxy is, the faster it moves away from us. You can see why this is using a balloon, a ruler and a marker pen. Inflate the balloon a little so that it is the size of a fist. Use the marker pen to make one fat dot and make three smaller dots in a line from the fat dot, each 1 cm apart. The first dot should be 1 cm away from the fat dot, and the third 3 cm away. Now fully blow up the balloon and measure the distances of the smaller dots from the fat dot. As the balloon is inflated, each small dot moves a different distance away from the fat dot – the farther away it is, the greater the distance it travels in the same amount of time, meaning that it must be travelling faster.

Peering into space

Earth's atmosphere interferes with light from stars and distant galaxies. To gain a clear view of the Universe, telescopes have been sent into space. They have sent back some extraordinary images.

Hubble Space Telescope

The Hubble Space Telescope has been sending back stunning images since 1993.

This view of a tiny part of space taken by the Hubble Space Telescope shows thousands of distant galaxies.

The primary mirror is made of 18 hexagonal segments coated with gold to help it capture very faint light.

James Webb Telescope

From 2018 onwards, the James Webb Telescope will orbit Earth with a mission to observe far into space and capture the **formation of the first galaxies**.

When you look up at the night sky, the stars appear to twinkle. Twinkling is caused by Earth's atmosphere. As light passes through the atmosphere, it is **refracted by moving air**. The direction of the light is changed slightly in random directions. This makes the stars appear to constantly change position, blurring the image.

Seeing back in time

When measuring huge interstellar distances, scientists use a unit called **a light year**. This is the distance light travels in one year. The light from distant galaxies has taken millions or sometimes billions of years to reach us. This means that we are seeing them as they were in the distant past. By looking right out to distant objects, we are seeing almost to the start of the Universe. This image from the Hubble Space Telescope shows distant galaxies as they were

13 billion years ago.

TRY THIS

To see how light is affected by a moving substance, you'll need a glass bowl, a piece of aluminium foil, a pencil and a torch. Wrinkle the foil, place the bowl on top of it and half-fill the bowl with water. Turn off the lights and hold the torch above the bowl pointing down. Now tap the surface of the water with the pencil to get it moving. **How does the foil look after the water has been tapped?**

Are we alone?

Our planet Earth is the only place in the Universe that we know to have life. Some astronomers are looking for extraterrestrial intelligence, searching for places that might support life and listening out on radio telescopes for messages that may have been sent across the galaxy.

Exoplanets

Scientists think that most stars have their own solar systems, with planets in orbit around them. In 1995, a large Jupiter-like planet was discovered orbiting the star

51 Pegasi.

Thousands more have been discovered since, including Earth-like rocky planets.

The Goldilocks zone

Earth-like life can only exist on planets where there is **liquid water**. This means that, like Goldilocks' porridge, they must be

'not too hot, not too cold'.

The region around a star in which a planet would be at the right temperature for liquid water is called the **habitable zone**, or the **Goldilocks zone**.

Habitable zone

Too hot

Too cold

Seven

Earth-like planets have been discovered orbiting the small star TRAPPIST-1. Three of them are in the star's habitable zone.

Life on Europa

Jupiter's moon Europa has a **frozen icy crust**. Underneath the crust, scientists believe that there is an ocean **100 kilometres deep** (that's ten times deeper than the deepest ocean on Earth). Scientists think that Europa's ocean may contain life. NASA plans to send a spacecraft to land on the moon by 2031 in order to find out.

"Shhhh, no one has seen me"

Can you help?

The SETI@Home project, run by Berkeley University in California, USA, has linked up more than 9 million home computers across the world to search for

extraterrestrial communications.

Each computer processes data gathered by radio telescopes such as the Green Bank Telescope in West Virginia. Anybody with a home computer can sign up to help!

Quiz

1 Name **the planets** in our Solar System in order from **the closest to the Sun** to the farthest away.

2 **The seasons** are caused by
a) The Moon's gravity
b) The tilt of Earth's axis
c) Changes in the temperature of the Sun

3 **The planets orbit** the Sun in a shape called:
a) A circle
b) A spiral
c) An ellipse

1900 **2000**

4 Which of the following was not a **leap year?**

2016

5 When Mars and Earth are on **the same side** of the Sun, this is called
a) Conjunction
b) Opposition

6 A comet's tail

always points
a) Towards the Sun
b) Away from the Sun
c) In the opposite direction to the comet's direction of travel

7 What is the name of the **molten rock** on which

Earth's

tectonic plates

float?

8 From Earth, the Moon appears at

right angles

to the Sun.

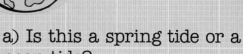

a) Is this a spring tide or a neap tide?
b) How will the Moon appear from Earth at this time?
i) New Moon
ii) Full Moon
iii) Quarter Moon

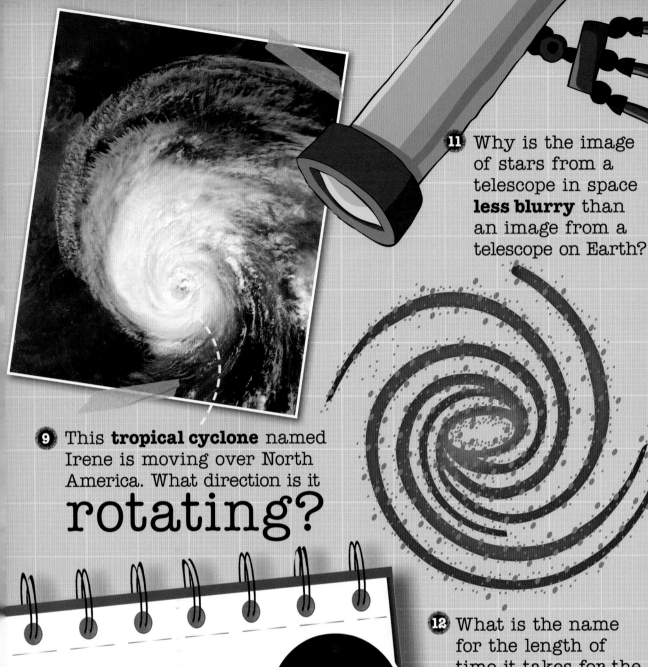

11 Why is the image of stars from a telescope in space **less blurry** than an image from a telescope on Earth?

9 This **tropical cyclone** named Irene is moving over North America. What direction is it

rotating?

10 This galaxy, named **EGS-zs8-1**, was discovered by a telescope in Hawaii in 2015. It is **13.1 billion light years away**. How many years are we seeing back in time in this image?

12 What is the name for the length of time it takes for the **Milky Way** Galaxy to complete one rotation?

13 What is the **estimated age** of the Universe?
a) 13.7 billion years
b) 13.7 million years
c) 200 billion years

Glossary

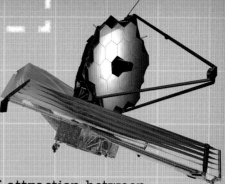

Black hole
A region in space that is so massive that nothing can escape its gravitational pull – even light is pulled into a black hole.

Coma
A cloud of dust and gas that surrounds a comet as it nears the Sun.

Condense
To change state from a gas to a liquid.

Eclipse
The partial or total blocking of light from one celestial body by another celestial body. A solar eclipse occurs when the Moon passes between the Sun and Earth. A lunar eclipse occurs when Earth passes between the Sun and the Moon.

Ellipse
A regular oval shape. The planets follow elliptical orbits around the Sun.

Exoplanet
A planet that orbits a star other than our Sun.

Fault
A place at which sections of Earth's crust move.

Galaxy
A system of millions or billions of stars that are held together by gravity. Most galaxies rotate around a central black hole.

Gravity
The force of attraction between objects with mass.

Light year
The distance light travels in one year. It is equal to 9.5 trillion kilometres.

Limestone
Rock made from the remains of sea creatures such as molluscs and coral.

Mantle
In the rocky planets, a region of molten rock between the solid inner core and the solid outer crust.

Parallax
The apparent movement of an object against its background due to a change in the position of the observer.

Radio telescope
A telescope that detects a form of invisible low-energy radiation called radio waves.

Refraction
The change in direction of light waves as they pass through substances such as Earth's atmosphere.

Tectonic plate
Solid pieces of Earth's crust that glide over the liquid mantle underneath.

Tropical cyclone
A large, rotating storm that forms over warm oceans.

Index

Answers

8. a) Neap tide b) Quarter Moon
9. The cyclone is in the northern hemisphere, so it is rotating in an anti-clockwise direction.
10. 13.1 billion years. This is the time it has taken the light to reach Earth.
11. Light is refracted by Earth's atmosphere, causing it to change direction, which blurs images from Earth's surface.
12. A cosmic year. It is equal to 250 million Earth years.
13. a)

1. Mercury, Venus, Earth, Mars, Jupiter, Saturn, Uranus, Neptune
2. b)
3. c)
4. a)
5. b)
6. b)
7. Magma